Love in the times of Pokemon

a collection of poems

Anurag minus verma

First published in India, 2017

A self-published book by Finer Things

Front Cover picture: Emile Séguin (Unsplash.com)

Printed at: Avdoot Printers, Mumbai

Author can be contacted at:

Conversations.anurag@gmail.com
facebook.com/conversations.anurag

Contents:

FULL HD EYES

I had a dream last night,

I was sitting in an empty classroom

of my college in the night

and two old pigeons,

strangely resembling

the pair present at

Baba Amarnath temple,

with torn out feathers

were sitting at the black window;

three benches ahead of

me, she was sitting and

all I could see about her

is her ponytail tied with

bright green band; swinging,

as she seemed busy writing something

she has always been busy,

whereas I have always had

all the free time in this world

to do any mundane thing:

like counting the blades of a running fan

or listening to the sounds of a house fly,

trapped inside the mug

or throwing grapes at wall lizards

or as these days,

watching pony tail

with bright green band

swinging

in a dream.

I wished my roll number was next to her's.

I wished my parents named me

Aanad, Akash or Ambani,

alphabet similar to her name,

so that I could have sat with her,

those days

and

this night.

the room was slowly filling up,

getting brighter

and in abrupt jump cuts, I was

moving one bench ahead at a time,

to reach right behind her.

I waited for a moment and

then gently took out her swinging green band

and she looked back

right at me with those

sad and mysterious eyes.

then something strange

happened and

in that dream,

I started

looking at

everything from her vision.

images of mine in her eyes,

were grainy, shaky and

low definition,

like a 144p video,

whereas the images

of the boy

dressed a bit too perfectly,

with a cold expression

sitting

next to her

appears

to be

in full HD

1080p.

now I know

that I need more clarity

in my thoughts

and in my image.

I hope one day

I'll become

a 1080p image,

immaculate,

crystal clear

and

high resolution;

getting

consumed

by her,

buffer free,

all day

and

all

night

long.

LOVE AND MOSQUITOES

whenever you are with me I feel like

I am high on coffee

or on some substance

which even kings crave for.

Is it the room purifier

or the smell of herbal mosquito repellent

applied on my leg

or the smell of perfume

applied on your body;

which I have once investigated

like a mad archaeologist scrutinizes

an ancient piece of

art.

I wish the feeling

which I am feeling

right now,

to stay a little longer;

a little longer than

it is going to stay

until you catch your flight

and disappear like

fading fragrance.

I wish the stories

of the destruction of the

world come true.

let the global warming do its job, right now,

let the cyclone approach,

let the comet hit,

or the moon fall on earth like apple

and let this be the

last moment on the earth.

The very last moment

of the human civilization,

where I am sitting at the airport coffee shop

looking at your body

and wondering

about a strange smell

emanating from somewhere.

I hear the cracking sound of

a mosquito getting electrocuted

by fluorescent Mosquito Killer Lamp

and wonder at the stupidity

of them flying towards the

machine again and again

only to get destroyed.

but then I accidentally

catch a glimpse of my reflection

in the mobile screen

and I look at

your eyes.

there is nothing much to talk here

just glances exchanged

now and then

and coffee being sipped

with uneven continuity.

how much I feel like

making out right now,

on this desk

tearing each other's clothes

while we smooch

and in the background

mosquitoes die,

more and more of them,

and this room full of people;

some of whom overwhelmed by the ecstasy of arrival

and some under the sadness of departure,

looks at us like

those mannequin

of the ancient world.

I come out of my reverie

as she touches my hair

and gives me

a last hug before saying

good bye with her lips which

now have become a little

bigger since

I last saw her 2 years ago.

she leaves

whereas I sit alone

at the table

sipping one more coffee

which now tastes

as bad as

ache.

I open my mobile

and check the

status of progress

scientists have made on

Einstein's theory of

General relativity

and then suddenly

feel a peculiar itch,

strangely at the spot

where I have applied

most of the herbal repellent cream.

what is there to write about?

poetry about flowers - Taken.

poetry about nature,

about life,

about love lost,

about the girl who left midway,

about missing the girl who left midway,

about depression,

about drinking,

(because the girl left)

about the terribleness of life,

about people,

about animals,

about dance,

about the ugly dance of life,

about an apple pie,

about blood oozing out of an apple pie,

about sudden melancholy,

about sudden death,

about a favorite song,

about boredom induced by repetition of a favorite song,

about remembering,

about forgetting,

about moons,

about nightmares,

everything is - Taken.

So, what should I write about?

or should I

write about

nothing.

This poem which I am writing,

is about horrors of being somewhere

in the middle of knowing

and not knowing,

at the same time

being possessed by a heavy dose

of confusion,

which might

be the only thing

one might

still write about

and is something

which is not yet taken.

a poet who knows no

shit about life

is very much close

to the minds of everyone else.

And finally, on this

foggy night, I am

glad that

I just

wrote one

which doesn't

suck that much

and it is

as much

confused as

you.

DRY DAY

The wine shop says that it's a dry day.

A Sikh god was born

about 900 years ago

and all alcohol shops are closed today

to celebrate his birthday.

God, does it again.

God doesn't want you to have a good time.

God doesn't want you to celebrate your tragedies.

A man on this foggy night is

cutting through the chilly winds

of the capital city,

one shop to another

in search of a beer,

to gulp down his loneliness

with a pack of chips

but no!

God, does it again.

God wants you to suffer,

like a bug inside a cobweb.

God doesn't want you to do nothing.

to do nothing in the world

so restless

and fast

is something.

to drink beer at home

on a Monday

afternoon is a statement

of protest against

capitalism,

mad speed

and career.

but no!

God, does it again.

I walk on the streets and see

some more people like me,

in search of a beer.

together we walk

like revolutionaries on a mission,

but soon

everyone gets dispersed

in different directions

like revolutionaries on a mission.

I am outside a bar

reading the menu

when the bouncer

comes near me

and says

"No sir. We don't allow

people wearing slippers

in our bar. "

I take a U-turn and

walk back wearing the same

slippers, of 9 number:

half-covered with mud

and rest in sadness.

I see an expensive bar,

where ladies with great legs,

smelling of good perfume

and men dressed in fine attires

smelling the good perfumes

of the ladies,

sit together,

chat

and laugh.

I enter it

and order the least expensive beer.

If you want to know

the real taste

of beer, you should

drink it on a dry day.

one gulp goes down

and its feels like

a pink flower

blooming near

your intestine.

sitting alone,

I take out my note book

and decide

to write a poem

as to not feel guilty

about spending so much

money on a single beer.

This poem costs 300 Rupees!

2:45 IN THE AFTERNOON

did nothing the whole day

apart from sitting in the bathtub

and playing with a paper duck.

now this boredom which is

piling up in every corner of the room

made him go out

and smoke a cigarette.

on the street at 2:45 in the noon

watching fleeting cars and fleeting faces,

as a young girl wearing

a grey aluminium colour of skirt,

with a white colour of top

came and stood next to him,

smoking a thin strawberry flavoured cigarette.

he pulled out his cigarette too

and mounted right between his lips

but the moment he blew out the first smoke

something extraordinary happened

as the smoke formed a shape

resembling a house with

a door and two windows

and it stood right above them

like a stuffy white cloud.

she looked at it and said in a relaxed tone

'Fascinating'

I asked her if she would like to come inside the smoke

and she responded by

throwing her cigarette

and stubbing with high heels.

I held her hand and we entered inside the cloud of smoke;

barren, smooth and calm.

milky, like waking inside a jar of molten white chocolate

as I could feel a tickle in the hair

because of the chilly wind blowing.

she walked with a mark of ecstasy on her face.

like an art lover visiting inside

the best museum in this world.

I asked her how she felt.

she didn't say anything and kept smiling.

I came near her and said,

"will you marry me?"

she didn't say anything and kept smiling.

a smile of discovering a lost world.

a smile of last man standing on earth.

she bounced on the floor and said-

"This is the best feeling I have

ever had at 2:45 in the afternoon"

I looked at her face;

calmness oozing out

beaming with bliss,

and at that moment I felt nice

for being the person who is making this girl feel so good

at that particular minute.

I checked out the watch and said

"the minute is ending, we must go back"

she stood up and we got out of the smoke

and loud traffic and all mundanity of daily life resumes.

she stroked my hair with her soft long fingers

before leaving the place.

I looked myself briefly in the mirror of the passing car.

there is something special about this day, I thought.

and while I was walking back towards my lonely room

I decided that

I should come out at 2:45 in the noon, often.

FUNGUS ON THE CHICKEN CURRY

There is a knock on the door

as lightning strikes on the blue sky

but very little

about anything

is dramatic here.

Life as stale

and static as last day

chicken curry

lying in the corner

abandoned by

cockroaches

and

even desperate

flies.

No one at the Door. It's only in your Mind.

Sleep baby, sleep.

You sleep.

a dream about

a girl who left you a few years ago

is back here riding her

scooter in dark mountains

in the skirt which you smelled

like a devotee once.

and in this white moonlit night

filled with sounds of wild peacocks

you follow her

shout, scream

then get tired

stop, drink water,

jerk off in the midway,

while fantasizing about the skirt

which you smelled like a devotee once

and you chase again

but she keeps on disappearing

and you keep on reducing

like an apple in the hand

of the hungry man.

She leaves one mile after another.

You die one inch after another.

you wake up with a bang.

Coca cola!

There is no such girl here. It's only in your Mind.

on the street,

smoking cigarette with coca cola.

girls everywhere.

hottest of them all are

tall one's wearing hot pants.

thank god

that summer exist.

some visuals to add on to the smoke

and for those 2 minutes

world seems

less frightening

until you go back to the room

stinking with

leftover

chicken curry

and nightmares

and lost hopes

and boredom.

I lay down on the bed

and the worst thing I see is

this 2-inch mosquito

which is right now

flying aimlessly

like an activist without an issue;

refuses to bite me

and abandons me

like that

chicken curry

lying in the

corner, alone.

WISH WE HAD MORE TO TALK ABOUT

2012, winters

you and me

in the coffee shop

and between us

that donut

which was too sweet,

90rs samosa

which was too bland,

and a cold silence,

which was why

sounds of chattering teeth

from the nearby table

were being overheard

with so much clarity.

I picked the newspaper and read out loud -

"look, Narendra Modi has won again in Gujarat.

Supreme court granted bail to 2G scam accused.

India has won against Australia.

heavy snowfall in Himachal.

weather is going to be worse here in Delhi too."

but you didn't respond to anything

and kept on looking at the

red back light of the car

blinking on and off

in the white fog.

wish we had more things to say

wish you were more aware of

politics,

world news,

history.

wish you took active interest in

philosophy,

poetry,

me.

It was so cold there that

I could see a smoke coming

out of your mouth,

mixing with

the smoke of this

hot cappuccino;

which you are not drinking,

just caressing on the

edges of its cup

with your slightly

broken nail of

2nd finger.

I took a sip of coffee

and to subdue the dead silence, said

I had a thought last night- 'What is life?'

answer to which I realised is this:

sometimes we are listening to a song,

a great song,

and how we wish the song should

never end.

you are into the groove, beats

and nostalgia where

the song is taking you through

but the ITunes clock is running as well

and it's moving towards the end.

you wish it to continue more

or maybe forever; never should this feeling end.

but it has to end,

the song from

very beginning

was actually

moving towards the end.

in between

beginning and end

are vibes, beats

nostalgia

but finally

it all ends.

song stops

and banality of life resumes.

you didn't respond to anything

and looked at the design of

heart made inside the coffee

and destroyed it gently

by taking a sip.

I offered you samosa

but you seemed low

and didn't eat anything

and I don't know what

it is that was

eating you from inside.

maybe you wanted to say something to me.

maybe words were just not coming out because of the cold.

how I wish you had something more to say.

how I wish there was less snow fall in Himachal.

It's 2016 now.

Trump is screwing up America.

a coup in Turkey has failed.

North Korea is conducting missile test.

United Kingdom is out of European league.

whereas I am sitting

in the coffee shop,

this time alone.

as fog collects

more and more

I begin to think that

what lies between us now

is a wall which is

bigger than the

one that

Donald Trump is ever going to build

and a distance

which no Narendra Modi

can ever travel.

28th December 2016

5:20 PM.

I am thinking about life in general

and a broken nail of

your 2nd finger.

the struggle of

the life shouldn't be

to fill up the bank account

or to reach at a certain

point in life which

some people call as 'growth'.

the struggle of life is

to maintain the innocence within you

and not to be embarrassed of being shy.

to be confused

and not to be embarrassed about having self-doubts.

to be vulnerable

and not to be embarrassed about being sensitive.

most of these qualities which we are born with

are too difficult to preserve

but more you go deeper,

more you'll know

that if there is something worth

preserving then this is it.

but it doesn't come easy,

as the more you'll grow,

the more people

will expect you to be 'Mature'

which is nothing but

a collective act of pretending

that now we have reached a stage

where we are finally living a valuable life.

it is a way of mocking your childhood self

by saying that it was devoid of any value

and whole life was designed to reach

at the stage which is called - Maturity.

but wise men will tell you that

life is not about reaching new stages

as there are no stages.

It's about knowing

that there isn't

much to know

and one shouldn't be proud of knowing

as there is nobody

who

knows

anything.

so next time you see

the picture of your childhood self

at some folder of your laptop

look closely at it.

the eyes,

at your eyes,

which were bright and full

and note how much of dullness

have crept within you

how much of cleverness have you allowed to enter

how much of shrewdness have made you to

calculate everything beforehand

how much of You is crumbling under weight of lies

which you tell yourself and others

each passing day.

and what about the peace

which all these so-called virtues

have promised us

where it has become difficult

to look at the morning flower for more

than a minute

without having

to worry about

the next impending deadline

or the bills that you need to pay

or the client whom you need to cheat

and the whole idea

about glorious growth

from child to mature

falls into pieces.

It must be still somewhere within you

and it's not too late to look out for it

and allow it to overwhelm you again

so that you can watch

the flowers growing for more than an hour

and may be eat its leaves as well

just to get the old kick

of knowing

how a rose taste

like these days.

A MADMAN DREAMS OF BEING REBORN AS A FLOWER

The days were passing like

random herds of pigs

passing into the butchering machine; killed, proceed

and then taken out in a basket

only to make space for the next pig.

Those days madhouses were filled with

people with wisdom and

some of the dim people

were there in schools

colleges, offices;

teaching people things

which were of

as much importance to them

as Michael Jackson

to white bears of the north pole.

One young man in the madhouse escaped

and started running naked on a crowded street

where nobody took any notice of him

as he raided the wine shops,

kissed and burnt all the bras,

clothes, shoes, creams, flowers and sunglasses

which were out on display for 50 percent sale.

He drank himself into oblivion,

laughed hard at everyone

and started jumping with joy,

while his head burst

in an explosion of this sudden joy

but instead of blood streams,

few butterflies came out of his head

flying randomly and sitting on the

beautiful girls wearing

cream-colored skirts

with red nail paint on their toe.

While he was lying down on the street,

with his head open like

a small roof top restaurant,

he shouted with joy;

"in this life,

I murdered my days

like stray cockroaches,

but, next time let me be born

like flowers which shine,

fresh and bright,

every day with

the light of

yellow sunshine.

INFERNO OF THE FIRST LOVE

She was 21 years old

I was 21 years old

I wanted to make love to her

She was waiting for me to make love to her.

and finally, we made love inside the car

parked at the corner of a busy lane.

some passer-by tried to look

inside the tinted black mirror

but we didn't care much

as we were possessed

by a strange dazzling energy

which only 21 years old

receive from

the makers of

this universe.

the explosion of emotions inside us

were beyond the mundane talks of

logic and rationality

and anything mattered

above all the other things

was to eat the flesh

of each other raw with love.

some called it game of hormones

some teen love

whereas others,

rightly so,

termed it as

inferno of first love.

She talked about patterns of her hair band.

I wanted to talk about Camus.

She liked Chocolate shakes.

I liked Rum with Coca-Cola.

She wanted a planned life.

I wanted the universe to end in 2012.

we couldn't find any common ground

except when we were

inside the car, making love

and it all felt as if the whole

universe was aligned

to make this event happen.

as if the big bang,

the battles,

constructions,

ideological revolutions,

political movements,

technological advancement,

earth moving around the sun restlessly,

everything so far, took place

to reach at that day

when I was inside the car

kissing the talcum neck of hers

as she clutched my shirt

and let me get the hold

of her breasts and

specially the soul.

her beautiful soul;

which mattered more

than anything

else.

after so many years

when I pass by that area

and look at the empty slot,

which was the witness

to the madness of love once,

I think about the nature of universe

among various other things

where events once happened

are never meant to be re- created again

no matter how much

you think about them

over the glass of rum

or try to pen them

in a poem.

somewhere in the

various corners of the world

there must be many 21year olds

consumed by the similar energy

and now it's up to them

to maintain the

necessary madness

in the world

which is crazy enough

to not lose its sanity

once in a while.

This one's is for them.

But especially for You!

he lived in the basement room

bereft of sunlight and sounds

and made friends with:

creaking fan,

four days old washed glass,

soap, spoons, slippers.

the beautiful stillness of everything was

enough to get him going

without doing much

in the room.

once in a while, he would venture out of his room to

play with children at the park,

have fun on the slides and seesaw

where no adult would have liked to have fun.

the old ladies sitting outside

their houses for

the winter sun

felt a particular kind

of disgust for him.

the thought of a man

playing with kids

on a Monday afternoon

instead of being

in the office

was enough for them

to consider him

as an object of hate

which became a talking

point among ladies

and soon they were all

united in hatred

and their evenings

turned more joyful

than they

were before.

he didn't specifically

had any purpose

or schedule of the day

and talking to someone

would be the last

the thing he ever wanted to do.

daughter of his landlord

liked his straight

long hairs which

according to her

reminded her

of an ex-boyfriend who

abused her most of the time

and she wanted to get

abused by him too.

but then he was

not very keen about

the proposal, as many things

in this world,

and gently refused

to divulge into

more such conversation

as he had to

go and feed

cats outside his room.

over the time his venturing

out of room became less frequent

and there were various theories

in the society, as to

why this person is

being alone in the room

'he is surrounded by philosophy books' said one

'I think he is a mad scientist working on ground-breaking
discovery' said another.

it had now have been a long time

since he stepped out of his room.

as days were getting converted into weeks

children, old ladies, cats,

all waiting for him

to appear out of the room.

finally, one day he came out of the house

looking pale and consumed by weariness.

his eyes looked puffy

which happens after

crying for too long

or may be staying awake for more than it is required to.

while he was walking towards the shop

children gathered around him

but he didn't respond

not even the smile

which he usually

had on his face.

old ladies for a moment

felt good about his return

but then they realised that something

is terribly wrong

and wanted to help him.

but he didn't want to be helped

and just wished to be

left alone.

a collective gloom

added to the winter fog

as cats cried in the corner.

there were theories

about what can be the reason

for his sudden slow destruction.

some said it was

lack of good diet and exercise

whereas some said

he might have possessed by the

spirit and must be taken

to the nearby temple to be cured.

but the most common

and the accurate

one was;

perhaps he is

one more guy

dying by knowing

too much about life.

out of nowhere these termites appear.

on the days when you are least expecting them

or on the day when you are sadly expecting them

and within no time they crawl inside

and soon they are everywhere.

all of a sudden, all meditation

yoga, antidepressant tea,

green smoothies, spiritual seminars,

crumble;

and you wonder

why am I the only

chosen one

but then you take a walk

on the street and see it

on the face of everyone.

on the faces of girls laughing in the bar,

on the face of a man waiting for the bus at the night,

on the face of a stranger asking for the address on the road,

on the face of people giving him directions on the road.

on the crushed paper inside the ATM rooms,

on the traffic lights blinking on the deserted

road after the heavy rain,

on the neglected red flower crushed by a speeding Mercedes.

inside the sound of the digital voice of Lift lady:

'please close the door'

inside the sound of early morning alarm clock in the empty house,

inside the sound of the sudden doorbell at midnight,

inside the sound of utensils dropping in the kitchen sink,

inside the sound of cockroaches being killed by a sandal,

inside the sound of car wiping blade in the rain,

inside the sound of the metal detector at the security check.

inside the notifications vibrations,

inside the fake chat smilies,

inside an oversaturated wedding picture,

inside the half-naked picture of the Instagram girl

selling towels.

inside the scary faces of chickens caged inside the moving van,

inside the happy faces of corporate employees moving inside the moving van.

inside the burning rocket taking off from the beer bottle,

inside the 3 people in uber share not talking to each other,

inside the green worm found in an exotic vegetable.

inside the scream of Russian Pornstars on laptop screens,

inside the stretched condom on the floor,

inside the ants marching around

the sperm drops under the chair.

inside the old lady sitting alone on the balcony,

inside a dog under the streetlamp,

listening to cries of a weeping cat.

inside the empty classroom in the night,

inside the ghosts at room 401,

where a lady died by

eating too much

of sleeping pills.

inside the lights getting dimmer in the room

inside the shadows getting shorter on the wall

inside the statue of laughing Buddha

staring back at you, mysteriously.

and then the people drink too much

on the weekend

and they all

vomits at the different

nook and corner of the city.

some of them hoping to kill termites

and some hoping to forget the existence of any such termites,

whereas somewhere

inside the wall cracks

of their spacious 2 BHK apartment

next set awaits,

to melt

into your

next day, quietly.

LOW BUDGET ROMANCE

it was a cheap and affordable romance

devoid of any pretence,

affluence,

or luxury.

the nation was suffering from

inflation,

price rise,

poverty,

economic gloom,

globalisation,

alienation,

people cribbing all the time

about all the things

but not they

as theirs was

a low budget romance.

expensive restaurants

tried to lure them with

large hoardings implying

you ain't in love

if you ain't treating your better half

at our fine dine restaurant

but they weren't amused

and ate at subsidized canteen

of their college,

as theirs was

a low budget romance.

they kissed in public libraries

hiding behind the books of

Dostoevsky and Lenin

and made love at

cheap government hostel roof

under the blanket of

stars and the moon.

they generally wanted

to make most out

of the things which were of low cost

like watching the sunlight changing in a park,

visiting a zoo once in a while,

making eye contact with a tree,

or sleeping in each other's arm

like entangled headphone wires

as the breeze from the balcony blew inside the room

which saved the Air condition bill

and kept room cold enough

and the romance,

reasonable enough.

TAKE IT

Take my arms

my liver

my intestine

my heart

my kidney

my balls.

Take it. Take it. Take it.

Take my dreams

my ambitions

my desires

my feelings

my romance

my lust

Take it.

Take my debit card

which contains 250 rs.

Take my old car which demands to

be pushed all the time.

Take my white cat which cries

like a dead child in the night.

Take my perfume which promised me lots of

girls but failed to get any.

Take my fairness cream which is as useless for me

as short skirts for Iranian girls.

Take my pride

my insecurity

my loneliness

fake ego

sleepless night.

Take it. Take it. Take it.

but leave this packet of chips right there.

I went to market all by foot on a

scorching afternoon to buy them.

she drops them at the table and says

'I'll not take it with me only if you promise

not to write such shitty poems again.'

I promise, I said.

she left and I waved her from the balcony.

then I quickly went into the room

and wrote this poem

while eating my favorite packet

packet of chips.

Infatuation

By looking deep into your mascara clad eyes

I can imagine a frame

worth 5043 Instagram likes.

Breakup

You now are nothing more

for me than a pixelated digital file

which is no

more available

for download.

where the cloud burst

and the child with grey hairs cries

till morning to the mid afternoon

where you couldn't figure out the dance of life

and things which were proven dull

are the things which you are into.

you cry on the bed

thinking about the injustice in the world

then thinking about the injustice done to you

and you cry more,

and your bed sheet made up of

velvet turns wet

you wash your face

and look in the mirror

at the face as dull as bad night

though there are some wondrous

things about aging

as aging is natural

but aging pathetically is

a waste.

The dream wounds

heroes die every day

popular heroes our only cultural elite

but one must understand that

a man walking on the street

getting the complexity of life

after suffering for so many years is a

hero.

A man lying on bed on a Monday afternoon is a

hero.

A man-eating 3 large scoops of ice cream after being

terribly ill is a,

hero.

A man who feels nauseated about life

and everything in general,

so much that on rainy days

wishes to be killed like a cockroach

but then due to a sudden change of heart

goes to the roof

and watches the moonlight,

smiles,

forgets everything,

and starts again,

is a hero.

FEELING LIKE

feeling like aging with you

bruised, broken, harmed,

torn, rotten but

still shining with you.

feeling like watching the time

passing by with you.

times of melancholy

distilled with the sadness of

the ages which just go

on and on

and we two are just another player

in this game till we disappear

and the same story is passed on

to another mortal in the same

format of

sadness

and

ecstasy.

feeling like disappearing with you

into the violet valley of nothingness

where we jump from one memory

to another

calm and unhurried

without having to worry about the

brutal rush of the time.

breaking all the rules of physics

and then laugh on the Newton

and then on the Freud

and then finally cry for hours.

feeling like to pack fragrance of your body

in an old rusted jar and then smell it

everyday.

feeling like to make purple midgets

with you from wet sand.

feeling like to eat clouds

alive with you.

feeling like to weave sweaters with you

from wool made from

sheep which dance

in a herd, post-midnight

under the white moonlight.

feeling like to tear cloths

feeling like to lick moon

feeling like to hear white sounds

feeling like to see naked mermaids

feeling like to meditate on pink flower

to drink

to jump

to blast

to evaporate

and

to become

the way

it was

always

meant to be.

SUNSHINE AND WICKEDNESS

Near sunshine river

at the time of sunset

two birds are sleeping

and snoring loudly.

A man in the nearby house

performing Buddhist meditation by

counting his breath

is trying to concentrate for 3 hours

but failing,

feeling irritated

and now this snore is making him crazy.

So crazy that he hallucinates that these

series of breaths are nothing but a

a violent attack on his nose

and he as a person is nothing

but a walking beast.

He takes out a gun from drawer

goes to the window and fires

An aimless shot.

Bullet flies

he cries.

In the nearby house

a girl is giving a blow job to a guy

for whom it is a historical moment

as he dreamt of this day

since the age of 12.

He always felt a strange layer of sadness

all his life and never knew

the reason of his existence

but this was the day when

all the ugliness of the world was dusting off,

a day when all the stars in the universe

are aligned at the perfect place,

when Vastu of the house is finally doing its job,

when all the grace of lord

is falling upon

this cranky room

smelling of stale food

and booze of last night.

He closes his eyes and all he can see

is golden sparks of light in the black background

but then the bullet enters the house

and goes right above girl's head

and gets out by piercing the wooden door.

girl gets terrified

and begins to cry

the boy rushes to wipes her tears

and while kissing her on the forehead to console her

he realized that he is

a luckless loser and

his life a series of endless misery

and that layer of sadness

that he thought for a while

is temporary

is as permanent as

a burnt cigarette wound

on the hand.

The bullet is aimlessly flying

near a jungle where

a backpacker girl

is sitting alone

near a bonfire.

Today is the date when she

was born 18 years ago

and wanted to celebrate by having

the first adventure of her life which

she never had a chance to have

all thanks to her classmates

who use to bully her

for having too much facial hair

and teachers defined her as

the dumbest person alive in the classroom

because she couldn't write the

correct spelling of the word - Rationality.

This is the day for this

universally rejected girl

when she is finally out and

traveling alone in the jungle

to find some answers.

The bullet pierce right above her ears

and passes blazing.

she hears the sound

and gets scared for a while

before getting back to the senses and

realizing an important thing

about the fickleness of the

human life and how it can end anytime

anywhere

without any hint

of rationality.

"Life has the layer of death all around it"
and with this thought, she realized that finally, she has
discovered something
which is deep and
profound and
has the value
akin to becoming
a Facebook status.

With this sudden entrance of profoundness
she sits on the rock
laughs out hysterically
like never before.

So loud was the laughter that it wakes up
those two snoring birds.

One bird yawns and says

"I had a strange dream right now".

'What dream?"

'Would you want to listen?"

'Yes' said the other bird.

The bird start narrating its dream

as the sun is getting diffused

under the cloud.

DEATH BY CHOCOLATE

a couple is eating chocolate truffle

which reminds me of our Chocolate Truffle

which we once ate

when the early summer

sun ray fell on half of your face

and another half of you looked as dark

as the night

when I am

writing

this poem

while drinking

in a cheap bar.

wish we could have become

two tiny bugs swirling

inside the chocolate truffle.

playing together

dying together.

Dying;

which seems

so much beautiful

than the life where

days of uselessness

are converting into evenings

of emptiness

linked by

way too much unorganized

thoughts which

are speeding aimlessly in my

head like cars with drunk drivers

post-midnight

and suddenly there

is a traffic jam

and horns

and honking

and fights

and road rage

and google map bleed red

whereas you are right

there in the middle of the road

eating a chocolate truffle

as black chocolate, slowly

melts towards

your chin.

even the happy hour in the bar

doesn't feel

happy anymore

and this beer feels like

a lie.

bar lights turn dimmer

and in the front of me

an orchestra lady sings

a song about memories

in a voice, so bad

that it took

away all the

sweetness of

honey potatoes.

outside the gate

I can still see couple

eating a chocolate truffle

and I feel like

walking up to them

and tell about

the moment they

are living now

is a nostalgia in making

and soon it'll

come to haunt

one of them

in its full glory

I somehow chucked the idea

and instead took

another sip of the beer

and wondered

why some people

call chocolate truffle

by the name-

Death by Chocolate.

SADNESS OF BUILDINGS AFTER RAIN

On a rainy night

a mosquito flies speedily

to crash at my ear and for a second

it feels like a plane crashing to suicide

at the twin towers.

I slap myself;

something I wanted to do

since quite some days

but didn't find any rational reason

to do so.

A fat mosquito

with well do to family

died for doing his duty

and created a blood dot on my ear

and I, while looking myself in the mirror,

reached to a lazy conclusion that

the violence of my thoughts inside my head

are nearly as gruesome as

the violence outside,

and that I, with blood on my ear

look as ugly as I

without it.

I walk outside and see the rains

which now have almost stopped

I scan my eyes around

and see line of houses

looking glum post rain.

I see sadness at the houses

where all the

people now

are sound asleep.

How can a building look sad

when people are sleeping peacefully

or even if they are having nightmares.

how all of a sudden everything feels

as gloomy as passing time

where even flowers look like dead child

the sound of cold breeze sounds like

an old woman crying in an apartment alone

the sound of water dripping on leaves

sounds like a cat getting electrocuted

by a naked

wire under the billboard

of 'Open happiness'.

I come back to the sofa where I was sitting

and think that

why everyone has to go through these kinds of days.

why the air of sudden melancholy creeps in

out of nowhere

like an annoying mosquito.

Readers, haven't you been inside one of these days?

MULTI-STORY APARTMENT

A parrot caged in the flat next to mine

speaks like a little boy sometimes

and if you don't give much

attention then you

might believe

that

you

just

heard

a baby

cry.

In the Apartment opposite to mine

a rich lady plays kickboxing

in the evening,

as her young maid stands there,

holding the glass of

green smoothies,

looking at the

the sky sometimes,

or at carefree pigeons

most of the time.

In another apartment

an Old lady who lives alone

watches Comedy Nights with Kapil everyday

but she never laughs.

Maybe it's difficult for her to laugh.

Maybe it's her teeth

which are placed inside the

scratched plastic bowl

kept on the table

besides a half cut

apple which

is getting rotten

with each passing minute.

As the old lady

changes the channel

from Kapil Sharma to news channel,

she waits for the

news of her

death, flashing live on

every channel:

One more old lady died

in an apartment, alone.

she half smiles as

the rotting apple is about to fall down from table

because of the vibration of her

chattering teeth.

In the apartment below her

a Chinese lamp glows dimmer

which lights up an abstract

Pahadi painting of Radha Krishna.

A girl enters the room, dressed in a glittering party wear.

She crosses the lamp

and for the blink of the second

the room turns dark.

She opens her blazer and throws it away

She takes off her heels and throws it away, too.

A man enters and he throws his red dotted tie on the bed.

As she is in front of the mirror

taking out her jewellery,

one by one.

He comes behind her

and shouts something

way too close to her ears.

she turns back

and slaps him on his face

and he in return slaps her back.

She punches hard on his chest

and tears out the pocket

of his white shirt.

He grabs her hairs,

she kicks him on his leg

and throws her high heels

which misses its target

and hits the Chinese lamp

which makes them silent for a while.

As they are looking at each other furiously,

she jumps on him and exchange a tight smooch

and he tears back of her glittering dress.

As they fall on the bed together

to make animalistic love,

the Chinese lamp

dropped on the table

blinks on

and off.

Slowly all apartment lights turn off, one after another

and only light which falls on it

is of the moon

which rises right above it.

Is it the size of the moon

or the size of the apartment

that it feels

way too near

as if

it can fall down on the

apartment

anytime soon

like one of those

Chinese lamp

and it may

awake parrot

sleeping inside

the cage, dreaming silently

after day's work.

When I was playing badminton at my hostel playground

I saw a boy entering the hostel escorted with his parents

who seemed to me about 15 years of age; slightly

chubby, fair skinned

but there was something about

his lips which were quite unusual

as they were pink and very big in size.

My badminton partner hit a smash and said-

"Another new admission"

During the evening, I was sitting in the common mess

where everyone used to eat food together.

In the background, an old Hindi song played

for which everyone shared a common hatred.

I saw him at bench next to mine with a

plate of rice and dal.

People near him were chatting and laughing

but he was eating his food, quietly.

1st day in the hostel carries a sentimental quality

when most of the boys go to their

room and cry under the pillow.

I sensed a similar kind of first-day expression on his face.

His room number was 109, which was next to mine

and as I was about to enter the room,

I saw him walking silently in the corridor.

I was sure that he'll cry tonight like I did on my first day

and with this thought, I attached the hard drive

to my laptop and watched porn to kill the long night.

A week later my room partner

barged into the room and said

"do you know this guy in the next room? "

I said what happened.

He said he organizes a smooch fest kind of thing.

I said, "smooch fest kind of thing?"

Yes. He said. Senior boys come to his room and smooch
him and in return, he charges 40 rs.

I said but why do boys smooch him?

He said because he has such smooth skin

and his lips are pink and juicy.

I looked at his face while he was describing it.

He remained silent for a second.

Then he said:

Disgusting. Yuck!

Late in the night as I was walking in the corridor

I saw few boys standing outside the room 109.

Chattering and giggling.

Entering inside one by one.

Coming out one by one.

I overheard the boys waiting outside the room

They were discussing what drama they are

going to perform for school annual function this year.

Boy in white said: I am going to take part in the play where Swati is playing the role of the maid. What Boobs!

Boy in Red said: do you know Swati comes to the school one hours before class starts.

Boy in white said: Why?

He replied "Because she meets her boyfriend

there in the empty classroom

and that's why her boobs have increased exponentially

in last two months."

As they were discussing a boy came out of the room

and he asked the boys who were waiting

to enter inside.

At the mess, I saw pink lip boy eating

food with few boys.

They were chatting to him

and he was listening to them

without speaking anything

eating rice and dal, indifferently.

Late in the night, I was roaming in the corridor.

I heard someone saying:

Do you have a cigarette?

There he was.

I for a while thought

isn't it unethical to smoke with a 15-year-old boy.

but then we went to the hidden area of our hostel.

We were smoking in silence.

Sharing one cigarette which was passing

from his lips to mine.

I looked at his lips

they were very pink and pulpy indeed.

Not a single trace of hair on his body.

I looked at his eyes which were cold and numb.

I wondered what story lies behind these eyes.

I wondered how many frustrated people came to his room

for a girlfriend experience.

I felt something odd about the way world functions.

He asked which film is releasing tomorrow.

I said I have to check in the newspaper.

He asked will you come with me

because I don't have many friends here.

I said, but there are lot many people

who come to your room.

He passed the cigarette to me

and after a brief silence said,

but they are not my friends.

I replied I'll see the name

of the film in the newspaper.

We both walked towards our room.

There were 2 boys outside his room

waiting for him.

They both smiled at the Pink lip boy

and he went with them in the room

after waving me bye.

I returned to my room.

I wondered why exactly this boy needs money?

Is it because of the money or he does it to kill boredom?

I picked up the newspaper and

started searching for movie name for tomorrow's show.

LOVE IN THE TIME OF POKEMON

the newness of the city,

the smell of used sheets,

the dampness of the room,

the fan which creaks too much,

and the walls which are too thin

that they can fall down anytime

and I might be one of those unemployed people

who are found dead in the hotel of the new city.

such thoughts of being dead

in such a sad cloudy day

makes me open Pokemon app

and catch a rare Pokemon which is

situated at 600 meters

from my hotel.

almost 100 people on the spot

with mobile in their hand

searching for the rare Pokemon

which will give purpose

to the everyday randomness

of their life.

I too become one of them

and start searching for one

through my mobile screen

but instead of Pokemon

I see a face

which I never thought I 'll see again, ever;

at least not in this sad cloudy day.

but here she is,

dressed in a black polo t-shirt

on the collar of which

the curl of her hairs,

resting.

and those eyes;

inquisitive

yet so cold.

should I walk up to her

or should I just run away?

what's there to talk after 5 years?

also, this is not the perfect shirt

and I forgot to apply the perfume

which I bought from the mall last night.

as I am struggling with the barrage

of thoughts, she notices me

and with the smile comes forward

and the crowd in the background cheers boisterously

as someone has found a rare Pokemon.

she stands next to me and says

'Oh my-my'.

I smile back.

as we hug each other

I smell a

peculiar smell

emanating from her body

which is something I am

the connoisseur of.

she tells me about HR meeting

for which she came here

and how much she will miss

the weather of the city

when she will be back to

her office, tomorrow morning.

I had nothing much to add up to it

so to reduce the

impact of this

sudden meet

and the awkwardness

which it has brought -

'Beers?' I ask.

she nods

and we go to

a nearby bar

illuminating with neon sign - Addiction.

it's the evening time.

songs on speakers connected to windows desktop,

sounds of chattering

mixing with

the fizz of beer bottles opening.

as she is sitting right opposite to me

I try my best not to have

any eye contact with her

and instead look at

the TV playing

the scene of a building getting demolished, slowly.

as I know very

well that If I look at her eyes

more than 120 seconds,

the time will suddenly slip

by 5 years

where the amount of my love

for her eyes

was such that

I made it

my wallpaper

on windows XP desktop

which later I sent to

the recycle bin;

an image lost in

whirlpool of the digital binary world

as she was lost in the

vortex of impermanence

of this world.

Not today.!

I don't want to lose all the

knowledge of Meditational Seminars.

All the knowledge of YouTube videos:

'How to Unlove- 5 SIMPLE WAYS TO FORGET HER'.

those books on Psychology and Science of Love.

all those empires of delusion

which I built all those years;

by saying myself that it's just a psychological image that

I am in love with not the original human being,

as these thoughts crashes in my head

my heart starts racing,

not in the dramatic sense of a way

but more in a medical sense of a way

as I have to put hands

on my chest to

control the racing heart.

so how it all went? - She asks

you tell me-I reply.

as she is talking about mundane things,

I notice few things about her that didn't change:

her way of rolling tongue on her dry lips after every 1 and
a half seconds.

her way of adjusting her hairs by holding the rubber band

in the mouth.

her way of touching under her ears every now and then

and all the other details that I meticulously noticed once

and made small notes of in my mind's diary.

I look at the clock

the night will end in some time

and how anxious I am about the speed

with which earth is revolving around the sun

as if for the first time I can feel being

on the planet- which revolves,

the time - which races

and human soul - which aches.

she is eating peanut masala and offers me some

but I don't feel like looking at food

and even the smell of my favorite

Chicken 65 cooked in

fresh garlic and curry leaves

from the nearby table

is not capable enough of attracting my attention

as every second of this night is devoted

to this strange irresistible

mad mad energy

which she had bought

along with her

and is

destructing me

slowly

minute by minute

like the building

inside the TV.

beer finally does its job

and she finally opens

about her life.

she talks about

the boyfriend whom she was so

madly in love with

that she wants to get married

but he at the last moment

walked out stating his

inability to indulge in any

such social responsibly

and this left her so

much broken that

she nearly went into

depression

and even attempted

suicide on Facebook live

to gain the sympathy of him

but even that didn't move him in any way

"As he knew very well that I

can never kill me

as I am the person

who can't even kill a mosquito

in fear that blood might

come out of it.

he knew so much about me - in and out.

but then one day he told me that

knowing too much about someone

kills all the thrill about

mad discovery in love

and the love

by definition

demands a certain degree of delusion

and belief in magic ".

more beers arrive on the table

as I watch at the college students

sitting at the table celebrating a birthday

but my mind can't seem to be fixed anywhere

and all I want now

is to cross this

one- table -distance between us

and lick the perfume

out of her body.

as the evening grows,

bar lights turn dimmer

and there is an announcement

about karaoke night

which makes us go out of the bar

where we decide to buy more beers

and drink it in the hotel room of mine.

while walking towards the room

my anxiety level about

time passing in such

a faster rate increases

and which makes me to thinks about 5 scientific

signs of being in love which I read in a book:

Loss of appetite

Mood swings

Separation anxiety

Craving

Intense motivation for emotional union

Possessive

Intrusive thinking

Damn close!

she sits on the balcony

looking at the moon

which slowly

appears out of clouds

as she takes another sip of beer

she asks

"Are my boobs small'

- "What kind of question is this "I reply

- "Tell me honestly"

- "I am not going to answer it"

- "Please"

- "They are Okay"

- "What okay?"

- "I think there is no problem with it. "

- "I think it's the extra fat on my body

which I'll take care of by joining the

Zumba classes in the morning

followed by the Ketogenic Diet.

Will he then come back? "- She says.

"You are too drunk now.

there is no problem with you.

You are still as beautiful as you were

and you have no idea how much

I mis…"

"why can't he feel with the same intensity as I do.

why can't two people watch the same kinds of dream

in the night, together.

like I am watching this moon above these city lights

which is making me feel something.

I want to share the same ecstasy

but no matter how close the other person is

he'll interpret it in a different way.

I can see his soul.

why can't he see mine? "

all the weight of those years

which have piled up into

minutes, days, week, years

are right here unfolding in the

- Hotel Supreme Heritage,

where two people watching a separate dream together,

are walking through

their own nightmares

and I wonder that

from the weight

of the collective loneliness

in the room

the building will collapse

and we would

be just another

2 people of the world

dead

by the

volcano of love.

About the author

Anurag minus verma is also a filmmaker and Video Editor, besides being a poet and a failed computer engineer. After completion of his Masters in Arts and Aesthetics from Jawaharlal Nehru University (JNU, Delhi) he went to pursue a course in filmmaking from FTII, Pune. Some of his films have been shown at various film festivals across the world.

He has a deep interest in poetry writing/reading. In his writings, he tries to incorporate various themes of urban existence marked by isolation, loneliness, randomness, humour in tragedy, love, nostalgia among various others.

Thank you himanshu kamble and Deba for proofreading poems of this book.

17826531R00079

Printed in Poland
by Amazon Fulfillment
Poland Sp. z o.o., Wrocław